Dream Big
Start Small
Achieve Success

Order Book
for Small Business

NAME   : _____

BUSINESS : _____

PHONE   : _____

EMAIL   : _____

BOOK NO : _____   DATE : _____

MODERN BIZ PRESS

Order Reference

✓	ORDER NO	DATE	ORDER NAME	PAGE
☐				
☐				
☐				
☐				
☐				
☐				
☐				
☐				
☐				
☐				
☐				
☐				
☐				
☐				
☐				
☐				
☐				
☐				
☐				
☐				
☐				
☐				
☐				
☐				
☐				
☐				
☐				
☐				
☐				
☐				
☐				
☐				
☐				
☐	ORDER NO	DATE	ORDER NAME	PAGE

Order Reference

✓	ORDER NO	DATE	ORDER NAME	PAGE
☐				
☐				
☐				
☐				
☐				
☐				
☐				
☐				
☐				
☐				
☐				
☐				
☐				
☐				
☐				
☐				
☐				
☐				
☐				
☐				
☐				
☐				
☐				
☐				
☐				
☐				
☐				
☐				
☐				
☐				
☐				
☐	ORDER NO	DATE	ORDER NAME	PAGE

Order Reference

✓	ORDER NO	DATE	ORDER NAME	PAGE
☐				
☐				
☐				
☐				
☐				
☐				
☐				
☐				
☐				
☐				
☐				
☐				
☐				
☐				
☐				
☐				
☐				
☐				
☐				
☐				
☐				
☐				
☐				
☐				
☐				
☐				
☐				
☐				
☐				
☐				
☐				
☐				
☐	ORDER NO	DATE	ORDER NAME	PAGE

Order Form

ORDER NO:

DATE:

ORDER NAME:

✓

Customer Details

Name :

Company:

Phone:

Email :

Address:

Order Details

	#	Item/Description	Qty	Price	Discount	Total
☐						
☐						
☐						
☐						
☐						
☐						
☐						
☐						
☐						
☐						

TOTAL

Payment Details

Order :

Shipping :

Discount :

TAX :

Date

Total

Status
☐ Paid ☐ Half Paid ☐ Pending

Payment Method
☐ Cash ☐ Credit Card ☐ Bank ☐ PayPal
☐ Other :

Special Notes

Delivery Details

Delivery Date :

Method : ☐ Pick-up ☐ Delivery

Tracking No

Status
☐ Started ☐ Finished ☐ Delivered

Order Form

ORDER NO:

DATE:

ORDER NAME:

✓

Customer Details

Name :

Company:

Phone: Email :

Address:

Order Details

	#	Item/Description	Qty	Price	Discount	Total
☐						
☐						
☐						
☐						
☐						
☐						
☐						
☐						
☐						
☐						

TOTAL

Payment Details

Order   :

Shipping :

Discount :

TAX   :

Date

Total

Status
☐ Paid   ☐ Half Paid   ☐ Pending

Payment Method
☐ Cash   ☐ Credit Card   ☐ Bank   ☐ PayPal
☐ Other :

Delivery Details

Delivery Date :

Method   :   ☐ Pick-up   ☐ Delivery

Tracking No

Status
☐ Started   ☐ Finished   ☐ Delivered

Special Notes

Order Form

ORDER NO:

DATE:

ORDER NAME:

✓

Customer Details

Name : _____

Company: _____

Phone: _____

Email : _____

Address: _____

_____

Order Details

#	Item/Description	Qty	Price	Discount	Total
☐					
☐					
☐					
☐					
☐					
☐					
☐					
☐					
☐					
☐					

TOTAL

Payment Details

Order : _____

Shipping : _____

Discount : _____

TAX : _____

Date

Total

Status

☐ Paid ☐ Half Paid ☐ Pending

Payment Method

☐ Cash ☐ Credit Card ☐ Bank ☐ PayPal

☐ Other : _____

Delivery Details

Delivery Date : _____

Method : ☐ Pick-up ☐ Delivery

Tracking No

Status

☐ Started ☐ Finished ☐ Delivered

Special Notes

Order Form

ORDER NO:

DATE:

ORDER NAME:

✓

Customer Details

Name :

Address:

Company:

Phone:

Email :

Order Details

	#	Item/Description	Qty	Price	Discount	Total
☐						
☐						
☐						
☐						
☐						
☐						
☐						
☐						
☐						
☐						

TOTAL

Payment Details

Order :

Shipping :

Discount :

TAX :

Date

Total

Status
☐ Paid ☐ Half Paid ☐ Pending

Payment Method
☐ Cash ☐ Credit Card ☐ Bank ☐ PayPal
☐ Other :

Special Notes

Delivery Details

Delivery Date :

Method : ☐ Pick-up ☐ Delivery

Tracking No

Status
☐ Started ☐ Finished ☐ Delivered

Order Form

ORDER NO:

DATE:

ORDER NAME:

✓

Customer Details

Name :

Address:

Company:

Phone:

Email :

Order Details

	#	Item/Description	Qty	Price	Discount	Total
☐						
☐						
☐						
☐						
☐						
☐						
☐						
☐						
☐						
☐						

TOTAL

Payment Details

Order   :

Shipping :

Discount :

TAX   :

Date

Total

Status

☐ Paid   ☐ Half Paid   ☐ Pending

Payment Method

☐ Cash   ☐ Credit Card   ☐ Bank   ☐ PayPal

☐ Other :

Delivery Details

Delivery Date :

Method   :   ☐ Pick-up   ☐ Delivery

Tracking No

Status

☐ Started   ☐ Finished   ☐ Delivered

Special Notes

Order Form

ORDER NO:

DATE:

ORDER NAME:

✓

Customer Details

Name :

Company:

Phone: Email :

Address:

Order Details

#	Item/Description	Qty	Price	Discount	Total
☐					
☐					
☐					
☐					
☐					
☐					
☐					
☐					
☐					
☐					

TOTAL

Payment Details

Order   :

Shipping :

Discount :

TAX   :

Date

Total

Status

☐ Paid   ☐ Half Paid   ☐ Pending

Payment Method

☐ Cash   ☐ Credit Card   ☐ Bank   ☐ PayPal

☐ Other :

Special Notes

Delivery Details

Delivery Date :

Method   :   ☐ Pick-up   ☐ Delivery

Tracking No

Status

☐ Started   ☐ Finished   ☐ Delivered

Order Form

ORDER NO:

DATE:

ORDER NAME:

✓

Customer Details

Name :

Company:

Phone:

Email :

Address:

Order Details

	#	Item/Description	Qty	Price	Discount	Total
☐						
☐						
☐						
☐						
☐						
☐						
☐						
☐						
☐						
☐						

TOTAL

Payment Details

Order   :

Shipping :

Discount :

TAX   :

Date

Total

Status

☐ Paid   ☐ Half Paid   ☐ Pending

Payment Method

☐ Cash   ☐ Credit Card   ☐ Bank   ☐ PayPal

☐ Other :

Delivery Details

Delivery Date :

Method   :   ☐ Pick-up   ☐ Delivery

Tracking No

Status

☐ Started   ☐ Finished   ☐ Delivered

Special Notes

Order Form

ORDER NO:

DATE:

ORDER NAME:

✓

Customer Details

Name : _____

Company: _____

Phone: _____ Email : _____

Address: _____

_____

_____

Order Details

#	Item/Description	Qty	Price	Discount	Total
☐					
☐					
☐					
☐					
☐					
☐					
☐					
☐					
☐					
☐					

TOTAL

Payment Details

Order : _____

Shipping : _____

Discount : _____

TAX : _____

Date

Total

Status

☐ Paid ☐ Half Paid ☐ Pending

Payment Method

☐ Cash ☐ Credit Card ☐ Bank ☐ PayPal

☐ Other :

Special Notes

Delivery Details

Delivery Date :

Method : ☐ Pick-up ☐ Delivery

Tracking No

Status

☐ Started ☐ Finished ☐ Delivered

Order Form

ORDER NO:

DATE:

ORDER NAME:

✓

Customer Details

Name :

Company:

Phone:

Email :

Address:

Order Details

	#	Item/Description	Qty	Price	Discount	Total
☐						
☐						
☐						
☐						
☐						
☐						
☐						
☐						
☐						
☐						

TOTAL

Payment Details

Order :

Shipping :

Discount :

TAX :

Date

Total

Status

☐ Paid   ☐ Half Paid   ☐ Pending

Payment Method

☐ Cash   ☐ Credit Card   ☐ Bank   ☐ PayPal

☐ Other :

Delivery Details

Delivery Date :

Method : ☐ Pick-up   ☐ Delivery

Tracking No

Status

☐ Started   ☐ Finished   ☐ Delivered

Special Notes

Order Form

ORDER NO:

DATE:

ORDER NAME:

✓

Customer Details

Name :

Address:

Company:

Phone:

Email :

Order Details

#	Item/Description	Qty	Price	Discount	Total
☐					
☐					
☐					
☐					
☐					
☐					
☐					
☐					
☐					
☐					

TOTAL

Payment Details

Order :

Date

Shipping :

Total

Discount :

TAX :

Status

☐ Paid   ☐ Half Paid   ☐ Pending

Payment Method

☐ Cash   ☐ Credit Card   ☐ Bank   ☐ PayPal

☐ Other :

Delivery Details

Delivery Date :

Method : ☐ Pick-up   ☐ Delivery

Tracking No

Status

☐ Started   ☐ Finished   ☐ Delivered

Special Notes

Order Form

ORDER NO:

DATE:

ORDER NAME:

✓

Customer Details

Name :

Company:

Phone:

Email :

Address:

Order Details

#	Item/Description	Qty	Price	Discount	Total
☐					
☐					
☐					
☐					
☐					
☐					
☐					
☐					
☐					
☐					

TOTAL

Payment Details

Order :

Shipping :

Discount :

TAX :

Date

Total

Status
- ☐ Paid
- ☐ Half Paid
- ☐ Pending

Payment Method
- ☐ Cash
- ☐ Credit Card
- ☐ Bank
- ☐ PayPal
- ☐ Other :

Delivery Details

Delivery Date :

Method : ☐ Pick-up ☐ Delivery

Tracking No

Status
- ☐ Started
- ☐ Finished
- ☐ Delivered

Special Notes

Order Form

ORDER NO:

DATE:

ORDER NAME:

✓

Customer Details

Name :

Address:

Company:

Phone:

Email :

Order Details

	#	Item/Description	Qty	Price	Discount	Total
☐						
☐						
☐						
☐						
☐						
☐						
☐						
☐						
☐						
☐						

TOTAL

Payment Details

Order :

Shipping :

Discount :

TAX :

Date

Total

Status
☐ Paid ☐ Half Paid ☐ Pending

Payment Method
☐ Cash ☐ Credit Card ☐ Bank ☐ PayPal
☐ Other :

Special Notes

Delivery Details

Delivery Date :

Method : ☐ Pick-up ☐ Delivery

Tracking No

Status
☐ Started ☐ Finished ☐ Delivered

Order Form

ORDER NO:

DATE:

ORDER NAME:

✓

Customer Details

Name :

Company:

Phone:

Email :

Address:

Order Details

	#	Item/Description	Qty	Price	Discount	Total
☐						
☐						
☐						
☐						
☐						
☐						
☐						
☐						
☐						
☐						

TOTAL

Payment Details

Order :

Shipping :

Discount :

TAX :

Payment Method

☐ Cash ☐ Credit Card ☐ Bank ☐ PayPal

☐ Other :

Date

Total

Status

☐ Paid ☐ Half Paid ☐ Pending

Special Notes

Delivery Details

Delivery Date :

Method : ☐ Pick-up ☐ Delivery

Tracking No

Status

☐ Started ☐ Finished ☐ Delivered

Order Form

ORDER NO:

DATE:

ORDER NAME:

✓

Customer Details

Name :

Address:

Company:

Phone:

Email :

Order Details

	#	Item/Description	Qty	Price	Discount	Total
☐						
☐						
☐						
☐						
☐						
☐						
☐						
☐						
☐						
☐						

TOTAL

Payment Details

Order :

Shipping :

Discount :

TAX :

Date

Total

Status

☐ Paid   ☐ Half Paid   ☐ Pending

Payment Method

☐ Cash   ☐ Credit Card   ☐ Bank   ☐ PayPal

☐ Other :

Delivery Details

Delivery Date :

Method   :   ☐ Pick-up   ☐ Delivery

Tracking No

Status

☐ Started   ☐ Finished   ☐ Delivered

Special Notes

Order Form

ORDER NO:

DATE:

ORDER NAME:

✓

Customer Details

Name :

Address:

Company:

Phone:

Email :

Order Details

	#	Item/Description	Qty	Price	Discount	Total
☐						
☐						
☐						
☐						
☐						
☐						
☐						
☐						
☐						
☐						

TOTAL

Payment Details

Order :

Shipping :

Discount :

TAX :

Date

Total

Status

☐ Paid   ☐ Half Paid   ☐ Pending

Payment Method

☐ Cash   ☐ Credit Card   ☐ Bank   ☐ PayPal

☐ Other :

Delivery Details

Delivery Date :

Method : ☐ Pick-up   ☐ Delivery

Tracking No

Status

☐ Started   ☐ Finished   ☐ Delivered

Special Notes

Order Form

ORDER NO:

DATE:

ORDER NAME:

✓

Customer Details

Name :

Address:

Company:

Phone:

Email :

Order Details

☐	#	Item/Description	Qty	Price	Discount	Total
☐						
☐						
☐						
☐						
☐						
☐						
☐						
☐						
☐						
☐						

TOTAL

Payment Details

Order :

Shipping :

Discount :

TAX :

Date

Total

Status

☐ Paid   ☐ Half Paid   ☐ Pending

Payment Method

☐ Cash   ☐ Credit Card   ☐ Bank   ☐ PayPal

☐ Other :

Delivery Details

Delivery Date :

Method : ☐ Pick-up   ☐ Delivery

Tracking No

Status

☐ Started   ☐ Finished   ☐ Delivered

Special Notes

Order Form

ORDER NO:

DATE:

ORDER NAME:

✓

Customer Details

Name :

Company:

Phone:

Email :

Address:

Order Details

#	Item/Description	Qty	Price	Discount	Total
☐					
☐					
☐					
☐					
☐					
☐					
☐					
☐					
☐					
☐					

TOTAL

Payment Details

Order :

Shipping :

Discount :

TAX :

Date

Total

Status

☐ Paid ☐ Half Paid ☐ Pending

Payment Method

☐ Cash ☐ Credit Card ☐ Bank ☐ PayPal

☐ Other :

Delivery Details

Delivery Date :

Method : ☐ Pick-up ☐ Delivery

Tracking No

Status

☐ Started ☐ Finished ☐ Delivered

Special Notes

Order Form

ORDER NO:

DATE:

ORDER NAME:

✓

Customer Details

Name :

Address:

Company:

Phone:

Email :

Order Details

	#	Item/Description	Qty	Price	Discount	Total
☐						
☐						
☐						
☐						
☐						
☐						
☐						
☐						
☐						
☐						

TOTAL

Payment Details

Order :

Shipping :

Discount :

TAX :

Date

Total

Status

☐ Paid ☐ Half Paid ☐ Pending

Payment Method

☐ Cash ☐ Credit Card ☐ Bank ☐ PayPal

☐ Other :

Special Notes

Delivery Details

Delivery Date :

Method : ☐ Pick-up ☐ Delivery

Tracking No

Status

☐ Started ☐ Finished ☐ Delivered

Order Form

ORDER NO:

DATE:

ORDER NAME:

✓

Customer Details

Name :

Address:

Company:

Phone:

Email :

Order Details

#	Item/Description	Qty	Price	Discount	Total
☐					
☐					
☐					
☐					
☐					
☐					
☐					
☐					
☐					
☐					

TOTAL

Payment Details

Order :

Shipping :

Discount :

TAX :

Date

Total

Status

☐ Paid   ☐ Half Paid   ☐ Pending

Payment Method

☐ Cash   ☐ Credit Card   ☐ Bank   ☐ PayPal

☐ Other :

Delivery Details

Delivery Date :

Method : ☐ Pick-up   ☐ Delivery

Tracking No

Status

☐ Started   ☐ Finished   ☐ Delivered

Special Notes

Order Form

ORDER NO:

DATE:

ORDER NAME:

✓

Customer Details

Name :

Company:

Phone:

Email :

Address:

Order Details

	#	Item/Description	Qty	Price	Discount	Total
☐						
☐						
☐						
☐						
☐						
☐						
☐						
☐						
☐						
☐						

TOTAL

Payment Details

Order :

Shipping :

Discount :

TAX :

Date

Total

Status

☐ Paid ☐ Half Paid ☐ Pending

Payment Method

☐ Cash ☐ Credit Card ☐ Bank ☐ PayPal

☐ Other :

Special Notes

Delivery Details

Delivery Date :

Method : ☐ Pick-up ☐ Delivery

Tracking No

Status

☐ Started ☐ Finished ☐ Delivered

Order Form

ORDER NO:

DATE:

ORDER NAME:

✓

Customer Details

Name :

Company:

Phone:

Email :

Address:

Order Details

	#	Item/Description	Qty	Price	Discount	Total
☐						
☐						
☐						
☐						
☐						
☐						
☐						
☐						
☐						
☐						

TOTAL

Payment Details

Order :

Shipping :

Discount :

TAX :

Date

Total

Status

☐ Paid   ☐ Half Paid   ☐ Pending

Payment Method

☐ Cash   ☐ Credit Card   ☐ Bank   ☐ PayPal

☐ Other :

Delivery Details

Delivery Date :

Method : ☐ Pick-up   ☐ Delivery

Tracking No

Status

☐ Started   ☐ Finished   ☐ Delivered

Special Notes

Order Form

ORDER NO:

DATE:

ORDER NAME:

✓

Customer Details

Name :

Address:

Company:

Phone:

Email :

Order Details

	#	Item/Description	Qty	Price	Discount	Total
☐						
☐						
☐						
☐						
☐						
☐						
☐						
☐						
☐						
☐						

TOTAL

Payment Details

Order :

Shipping :

Discount :

TAX :

Date

Total

Status
☐ Paid ☐ Half Paid ☐ Pending

Payment Method
☐ Cash ☐ Credit Card ☐ Bank ☐ PayPal
☐ Other :

Special Notes

Delivery Details

Delivery Date :

Method : ☐ Pick-up ☐ Delivery

Tracking No

Status
☐ Started ☐ Finished ☐ Delivered

Order Form

ORDER NO:

DATE:

ORDER NAME:

✓

Customer Details

Name : _____

Address: _____

Company: _____

_____

Phone: _____

Email : _____

_____

Order Details

	#	Item/Description	Qty	Price	Discount	Total
☐						
☐						
☐						
☐						
☐						
☐						
☐						
☐						
☐						
☐						

TOTAL

Payment Details

Order : _____

Shipping : _____

Discount : _____

TAX : _____

Date

Total

Status

☐ Paid ☐ Half Paid ☐ Pending

Payment Method

☐ Cash ☐ Credit Card ☐ Bank ☐ PayPal

☐ Other : _____

Delivery Details

Delivery Date : _____

Method : ☐ Pick-up ☐ Delivery

Tracking No

Status

☐ Started ☐ Finished ☐ Delivered

Special Notes

Order Form

ORDER NO:

DATE:

ORDER NAME:

✓

Customer Details

Name :

Address:

Company:

Phone:

Email :

Order Details

	#	Item/Description	Qty	Price	Discount	Total
☐						
☐						
☐						
☐						
☐						
☐						
☐						
☐						
☐						
☐						

TOTAL

Payment Details

Order   :

Shipping :

Discount :

TAX   :

Date

Total

Status

☐ Paid   ☐ Half Paid   ☐ Pending

Payment Method

☐ Cash   ☐ Credit Card   ☐ Bank   ☐ PayPal

☐ Other :

Delivery Details

Delivery Date :

Method   :   ☐ Pick-up   ☐ Delivery

Tracking No

Status

☐ Started   ☐ Finished   ☐ Delivered

Special Notes

Order Form

ORDER NO:

DATE:

ORDER NAME:

✓

Customer Details

Name :

Company:

Phone:

Email :

Address:

Order Details

	#	Item/Description	Qty	Price	Discount	Total
☐						
☐						
☐						
☐						
☐						
☐						
☐						
☐						
☐						
☐						

TOTAL

Payment Details

Order :

Shipping :

Discount :

TAX :

Date

Total

Status
☐ Paid ☐ Half Paid ☐ Pending

Payment Method
☐ Cash ☐ Credit Card ☐ Bank ☐ PayPal
☐ Other :

Delivery Details

Delivery Date :

Method : ☐ Pick-up ☐ Delivery

Tracking No

Status
☐ Started ☐ Finished ☐ Delivered

Special Notes

Order Form

ORDER NO:

DATE:

ORDER NAME:

✓

Customer Details

Name :

Company:

Phone:

Email :

Address:

Order Details

	#	Item/Description	Qty	Price	Discount	Total
☐						
☐						
☐						
☐						
☐						
☐						
☐						
☐						
☐						
☐						

TOTAL

Payment Details

Order :

Shipping :

Discount :

TAX :

Date

Total

Status

☐ Paid   ☐ Half Paid   ☐ Pending

Payment Method

☐ Cash   ☐ Credit Card   ☐ Bank   ☐ PayPal

☐ Other :

Special Notes

Delivery Details

Delivery Date :

Method : ☐ Pick-up   ☐ Delivery

Tracking No

Status

☐ Started   ☐ Finished   ☐ Delivered

Order Form

ORDER NO:

DATE:

ORDER NAME:

✓

Customer Details

Name :

Address:

Company:

Phone:

Email :

Order Details

	#	Item/Description	Qty	Price	Discount	Total
☐						
☐						
☐						
☐						
☐						
☐						
☐						
☐						
☐						
☐						

TOTAL

Payment Details

Order :

Shipping :

Discount :

TAX :

Date

Total

Status

☐ Paid ☐ Half Paid ☐ Pending

Payment Method

☐ Cash ☐ Credit Card ☐ Bank ☐ PayPal

☐ Other :

Delivery Details

Delivery Date :

Method : ☐ Pick-up ☐ Delivery

Tracking No

Status

☐ Started ☐ Finished ☐ Delivered

Special Notes

Order Form

ORDER NO:

DATE:

ORDER NAME:

✓

Customer Details

Name :

Address:

Company:

Phone:

Email :

Order Details

	#	Item/Description	Qty	Price	Discount	Total
☐						
☐						
☐						
☐						
☐						
☐						
☐						
☐						
☐						
☐						

TOTAL

Payment Details

Order :

Shipping :

Discount :

TAX :

Date

Total

Status

☐ Paid ☐ Half Paid ☐ Pending

Payment Method

☐ Cash ☐ Credit Card ☐ Bank ☐ PayPal

☐ Other :

Delivery Details

Delivery Date :

Method : ☐ Pick-up ☐ Delivery

Tracking No

Status

☐ Started ☐ Finished ☐ Delivered

Special Notes

Order Form

ORDER NO:

DATE:

ORDER NAME:

✓

Customer Details

Name :

Company:

Phone:

Email :

Address:

Order Details

	#	Item/Description	Qty	Price	Discount	Total
☐						
☐						
☐						
☐						
☐						
☐						
☐						
☐						
☐						
☐						

TOTAL

Payment Details

Order :

Shipping :

Discount:

TAX :

Date

Total

Status

☐ Paid ☐ Half Paid ☐ Pending

Payment Method

☐ Cash ☐ Credit Card ☐ Bank ☐ PayPal

☐ Other :

Special Notes

Delivery Details

Delivery Date :

Method : ☐ Pick-up ☐ Delivery

Tracking No

Status

☐ Started ☐ Finished ☐ Delivered

Order Form

ORDER NO:

DATE:

ORDER NAME:

✓

Customer Details

Name :

Address:

Company:

Phone:

Email :

Order Details

	#	Item/Description	Qty	Price	Discount	Total
☐						
☐						
☐						
☐						
☐						
☐						
☐						
☐						
☐						
☐						

TOTAL

Payment Details

Order :

Shipping :

Discount :

TAX :

Date

Total

Status

☐ Paid   ☐ Half Paid   ☐ Pending

Payment Method

☐ Cash   ☐ Credit Card   ☐ Bank   ☐ PayPal

☐ Other :

Special Notes

Delivery Details

Delivery Date :

Method : ☐ Pick-up   ☐ Delivery

Tracking No

Status

☐ Started   ☐ Finished   ☐ Delivered

Order Form

ORDER NO:

DATE:

ORDER NAME:

✓

Customer Details

Name :

Address:

Company:

Phone:

Email :

Order Details

	#	Item/Description	Qty	Price	Discount	Total
☐						
☐						
☐						
☐						
☐						
☐						
☐						
☐						
☐						
☐						

TOTAL

Payment Details

Order :

Shipping :

Discount :

TAX :

Date

Total

Status
☐ Paid ☐ Half Paid ☐ Pending

Payment Method
☐ Cash ☐ Credit Card ☐ Bank ☐ PayPal
☐ Other :

Delivery Details

Delivery Date :

Method : ☐ Pick-up ☐ Delivery

Tracking No

Status
☐ Started ☐ Finished ☐ Delivered

Special Notes

Order Form

ORDER NO:

DATE:

ORDER NAME:

✓

Customer Details

Name :

Company:

Phone:

Email :

Address:

Order Details

	#	Item/Description	Qty	Price	Discount	Total
☐						
☐						
☐						
☐						
☐						
☐						
☐						
☐						
☐						
☐						

TOTAL

Payment Details

Order :

Shipping :

Discount :

TAX :

Date

Total

Status

☐ Paid ☐ Half Paid ☐ Pending

Payment Method

☐ Cash ☐ Credit Card ☐ Bank ☐ PayPal

☐ Other :

Delivery Details

Delivery Date :

Method : ☐ Pick-up ☐ Delivery

Tracking No

Status

☐ Started ☐ Finished ☐ Delivered

Special Notes

Order Form

ORDER NO:

DATE:

ORDER NAME: ✓

Customer Details

Name :

Company:

Phone: Email :

Address:

Order Details

	#	Item/Description	Qty	Price	Discount	Total
☐						
☐						
☐						
☐						
☐						
☐						
☐						
☐						
☐						
☐						
					TOTAL	

Payment Details

Order   :

Shipping :

Discount :

TAX   :

Date

Total

Status

☐ Paid   ☐ Half Paid   ☐ Pending

Payment Method

☐ Cash   ☐ Credit Card   ☐ Bank   ☐ PayPal

☐ Other :

Special Notes

Delivery Details

Delivery Date :

Method   :   ☐ Pick-up   ☐ Delivery

Tracking No

Status

☐ Started   ☐ Finished   ☐ Delivered

Order Form

ORDER NO:

DATE:

ORDER NAME:

✓

Customer Details

Name :

Company:

Phone:

Email :

Address:

Order Details

	#	Item/Description	Qty	Price	Discount	Total
☐						
☐						
☐						
☐						
☐						
☐						
☐						
☐						
☐						
☐						

TOTAL

Payment Details

Order :

Shipping :

Discount :

TAX :

Date

Total

Status
☐ Paid ☐ Half Paid ☐ Pending

Payment Method
☐ Cash ☐ Credit Card ☐ Bank ☐ PayPal
☐ Other :

Delivery Details

Delivery Date :

Method : ☐ Pick-up ☐ Delivery

Tracking No

Status
☐ Started ☐ Finished ☐ Delivered

Special Notes

Order Form

ORDER NO:

DATE:

ORDER NAME:

✓

Customer Details

Name :

Company:

Phone:

Email :

Address:

Order Details

	#	Item/Description	Qty	Price	Discount	Total
☐						
☐						
☐						
☐						
☐						
☐						
☐						
☐						
☐						
☐						

TOTAL

Payment Details

Order :

Shipping :

Discount :

TAX :

Date

Total

Status

☐ Paid   ☐ Half Paid   ☐ Pending

Payment Method

☐ Cash   ☐ Credit Card   ☐ Bank   ☐ PayPal

☐ Other :

Delivery Details

Delivery Date :

Method :   ☐ Pick-up   ☐ Delivery

Tracking No

Status

☐ Started   ☐ Finished   ☐ Delivered

Special Notes

Order Form

ORDER NO:

DATE:

ORDER NAME:

✓

Customer Details

Name :

Company:

Phone:

Email :

Address:

Order Details

	#	Item/Description	Qty	Price	Discount	Total
☐						
☐						
☐						
☐						
☐						
☐						
☐						
☐						
☐						
☐						

TOTAL

Payment Details

Order :

Shipping :

Discount :

TAX :

Date

Total

Status
☐ Paid ☐ Half Paid ☐ Pending

Payment Method
☐ Cash ☐ Credit Card ☐ Bank ☐ PayPal
☐ Other :

Delivery Details

Delivery Date :

Method : ☐ Pick-up ☐ Delivery

Tracking No

Status
☐ Started ☐ Finished ☐ Delivered

Special Notes

Order Form

ORDER NO:

DATE:

ORDER NAME:

✓

Customer Details

Name :

Address:

Company:

Phone:

Email :

Order Details

	#	Item/Description	Qty	Price	Discount	Total
☐						
☐						
☐						
☐						
☐						
☐						
☐						
☐						
☐						
☐						

TOTAL

Payment Details

Order :

Shipping :

Discount :

TAX :

Date

Total

Status

☐ Paid ☐ Half Paid ☐ Pending

Payment Method

☐ Cash ☐ Credit Card ☐ Bank ☐ PayPal

☐ Other :

Delivery Details

Delivery Date :

Method : ☐ Pick-up ☐ Delivery

Tracking No

Status

☐ Started ☐ Finished ☐ Delivered

Special Notes

Order Form

ORDER NO:

DATE:

ORDER NAME:

✓

Customer Details

Name :

Company:

Phone:

Email :

Address:

Order Details

#	Item/Description	Qty	Price	Discount	Total
☐					
☐					
☐					
☐					
☐					
☐					
☐					
☐					
☐					
☐					

TOTAL

Payment Details

Order :

Shipping :

Discount :

TAX :

Date

Total

Status

☐ Paid ☐ Half Paid ☐ Pending

Payment Method

☐ Cash ☐ Credit Card ☐ Bank ☐ PayPal

☐ Other :

Delivery Details

Delivery Date :

Method : ☐ Pick-up ☐ Delivery

Tracking No

Status

☐ Started ☐ Finished ☐ Delivered

Special Notes

Order Form

ORDER NO:

DATE:

ORDER NAME:

✓

Customer Details

Name :

Address:

Company:

Phone:

Email :

Order Details

	#	Item/Description	Qty	Price	Discount	Total
☐						
☐						
☐						
☐						
☐						
☐						
☐						
☐						
☐						
☐						

TOTAL

Payment Details

Order :

Shipping :

Discount :

TAX :

Date

Total

Status

☐ Paid ☐ Half Paid ☐ Pending

Payment Method

☐ Cash ☐ Credit Card ☐ Bank ☐ PayPal

☐ Other :

Delivery Details

Delivery Date :

Method : ☐ Pick-up ☐ Delivery

Tracking No

Status

☐ Started ☐ Finished ☐ Delivered

Special Notes

Order Form

ORDER NO:

DATE:

ORDER NAME:

✓

Customer Details

Name :

Address:

Company:

Phone:

Email :

Order Details

	#	Item/Description	Qty	Price	Discount	Total
☐						
☐						
☐						
☐						
☐						
☐						
☐						
☐						
☐						
☐						

TOTAL

Payment Details

Order :

Shipping :

Discount :

TAX :

Date

Total

Status
☐ Paid ☐ Half Paid ☐ Pending

Payment Method
☐ Cash ☐ Credit Card ☐ Bank ☐ PayPal
☐ Other :

Delivery Details

Delivery Date :

Method : ☐ Pick-up ☐ Delivery

Tracking No

Status
☐ Started ☐ Finished ☐ Delivered

Special Notes

Order Form

ORDER NO:

DATE:

ORDER NAME:

✓

Customer Details

Name :

Address:

Company:

Phone:

Email :

Order Details

	#	Item/Description	Qty	Price	Discount	Total
☐						
☐						
☐						
☐						
☐						
☐						
☐						
☐						
☐						
☐						

TOTAL

Payment Details

Order :

Shipping :

Discount :

TAX :

Date

Total

Status

☐ Paid ☐ Half Paid ☐ Pending

Payment Method

☐ Cash ☐ Credit Card ☐ Bank ☐ PayPal

☐ Other :

Delivery Details

Delivery Date :

Method : ☐ Pick-up ☐ Delivery

Tracking No

Status

☐ Started ☐ Finished ☐ Delivered

Special Notes

Order Form

ORDER NO:

DATE:

ORDER NAME:

✓

Customer Details

Name :

Address:

Company:

Phone:

Email :

Order Details

#	Item/Description	Qty	Price	Discount	Total
☐					
☐					
☐					
☐					
☐					
☐					
☐					
☐					
☐					
☐					

TOTAL

Payment Details

Order :

Shipping :

Discount :

TAX :

Date

Total

Status

☐ Paid   ☐ Half Paid   ☐ Pending

Payment Method

☐ Cash   ☐ Credit Card   ☐ Bank   ☐ PayPal

☐ Other :

Delivery Details

Delivery Date :

Method : ☐ Pick-up   ☐ Delivery

Tracking No

Status

☐ Started   ☐ Finished   ☐ Delivered

Special Notes

Order Form

ORDER NO:

DATE:

ORDER NAME:

✓

Customer Details

Name :

Company:

Phone:

Email :

Address:

Order Details

	#	Item/Description	Qty	Price	Discount	Total
☐						
☐						
☐						
☐						
☐						
☐						
☐						
☐						
☐						
☐						

TOTAL

Payment Details

Order :

Shipping :

Discount :

TAX :

Date

Total

Status

☐ Paid ☐ Half Paid ☐ Pending

Payment Method

☐ Cash ☐ Credit Card ☐ Bank ☐ PayPal

☐ Other :

Delivery Details

Delivery Date :

Method : ☐ Pick-up ☐ Delivery

Tracking No

Status

☐ Started ☐ Finished ☐ Delivered

Special Notes

Order Form

ORDER NO:

DATE:

ORDER NAME:

✓

Customer Details

Name :

Company:

Phone:

Email :

Address:

Order Details

☐	#	Item/Description	Qty	Price	Discount	Total
☐						
☐						
☐						
☐						
☐						
☐						
☐						
☐						
☐						
☐						
					TOTAL	

Payment Details

Order :

Shipping :

Discount :

TAX :

Date

Total

Status

☐ Paid ☐ Half Paid ☐ Pending

Payment Method

☐ Cash ☐ Credit Card ☐ Bank ☐ PayPal

☐ Other :

Special Notes

Delivery Details

Delivery Date :

Method : ☐ Pick-up ☐ Delivery

Tracking No

Status

☐ Started ☐ Finished ☐ Delivered

Order Form

ORDER NO:

DATE:

ORDER NAME:

✓

Customer Details

Name :

Address:

Company:

Phone:

Email :

Order Details

	#	Item/Description	Qty	Price	Discount	Total
☐						
☐						
☐						
☐						
☐						
☐						
☐						
☐						
☐						
☐						

TOTAL

Payment Details

Order :

Shipping :

Discount :

TAX :

Date

Total

Status

☐ Paid ☐ Half Paid ☐ Pending

Payment Method

☐ Cash ☐ Credit Card ☐ Bank ☐ PayPal

☐ Other :

Delivery Details

Delivery Date :

Method : ☐ Pick-up ☐ Delivery

Tracking No

Status

☐ Started ☐ Finished ☐ Delivered

Special Notes

Order Form

ORDER NO:

DATE:

ORDER NAME:

✓

Customer Details

Name :

Company:

Phone:

Email :

Address:

Order Details

	#	Item/Description	Qty	Price	Discount	Total
☐						
☐						
☐						
☐						
☐						
☐						
☐						
☐						
☐						
☐						

TOTAL

Payment Details

Order :

Shipping :

Discount :

TAX :

Date

Total

Status

☐ Paid ☐ Half Paid ☐ Pending

Payment Method

☐ Cash ☐ Credit Card ☐ Bank ☐ PayPal

☐ Other :

Special Notes

Delivery Details

Delivery Date :

Method : ☐ Pick-up ☐ Delivery

Tracking No

Status

☐ Started ☐ Finished ☐ Delivered

Order Form

ORDER NO:

DATE:

ORDER NAME:

✓

Customer Details

Name : _____

Company: _____

Phone: _____ Email : _____

Address: _____
_____

Order Details

☐	#	Item/Description	Qty	Price	Discount	Total
☐						
☐						
☐						
☐						
☐						
☐						
☐						
☐						
☐						
☐						
					TOTAL	

Payment Details

Order   : _____

Shipping : _____

Discount : _____

TAX   : _____

Date

Total

Status
☐ Paid   ☐ Half Paid   ☐ Pending

Payment Method
☐ Cash   ☐ Credit Card   ☐ Bank   ☐ PayPal
☐ Other :

Special Notes

Delivery Details

Delivery Date : _____

Method   : ☐ Pick-up   ☐ Delivery

Tracking No

Status
☐ Started   ☐ Finished   ☐ Delivered

Order Form

ORDER NO:

DATE:

ORDER NAME:

✓

Customer Details

Name :

Address:

Company:

Phone:

Email :

Order Details

#	Item/Description	Qty	Price	Discount	Total
☐					
☐					
☐					
☐					
☐					
☐					
☐					
☐					
☐					
☐					

TOTAL

Payment Details

Order :

Shipping :

Discount :

TAX :

Date

Total

Status

☐ Paid   ☐ Half Paid   ☐ Pending

Payment Method

☐ Cash   ☐ Credit Card   ☐ Bank   ☐ PayPal

☐ Other :

Special Notes

Delivery Details

Delivery Date :

Method : ☐ Pick-up   ☐ Delivery

Tracking No

Status

☐ Started   ☐ Finished   ☐ Delivered

Order Form

ORDER NO:

DATE:

ORDER NAME:

✓

Customer Details

Name :

Company:

Phone:

Email :

Address:

Order Details

	#	Item/Description	Qty	Price	Discount	Total
☐						
☐						
☐						
☐						
☐						
☐						
☐						
☐						
☐						
☐						

TOTAL

Payment Details

Order :

Shipping :

Discount :

TAX :

Date

Total

Status
- ☐ Paid
- ☐ Half Paid
- ☐ Pending

Payment Method
- ☐ Cash
- ☐ Credit Card
- ☐ Bank
- ☐ PayPal
- ☐ Other :

Special Notes

Delivery Details

Delivery Date :

Method : ☐ Pick-up ☐ Delivery

Tracking No

Status
- ☐ Started
- ☐ Finished
- ☐ Delivered

Order Form

ORDER NO:

DATE:

ORDER NAME:

✓

Customer Details

Name :

Company:

Phone:

Email :

Address:

Order Details

	#	Item/Description	Qty	Price	Discount	Total
☐						
☐						
☐						
☐						
☐						
☐						
☐						
☐						
☐						
☐						

TOTAL

Payment Details

Order :

Shipping :

Discount :

TAX :

Date

Total

Status
☐ Paid ☐ Half Paid ☐ Pending

Payment Method
☐ Cash ☐ Credit Card ☐ Bank ☐ PayPal
☐ Other :

Special Notes

Delivery Details

Delivery Date :

Method : ☐ Pick-up ☐ Delivery

Tracking No

Status
☐ Started ☐ Finished ☐ Delivered

Order Form

ORDER NO:

DATE:

ORDER NAME:

✓

Customer Details

Name :

Address:

Company:

Phone:

Email :

Order Details

☐	#	Item/Description	Qty	Price	Discount	Total
☐						
☐						
☐						
☐						
☐						
☐						
☐						
☐						
☐						
☐						

TOTAL

Payment Details

Order :

Shipping :

Discount :

TAX :

Date

Total

Status

☐ Paid   ☐ Half Paid   ☐ Pending

Payment Method

☐ Cash   ☐ Credit Card   ☐ Bank   ☐ PayPal

☐ Other :

Delivery Details

Delivery Date :

Method : ☐ Pick-up   ☐ Delivery

Tracking No

Status

☐ Started   ☐ Finished   ☐ Delivered

Special Notes

Order Form

ORDER NO:

DATE:

ORDER NAME:

✓

Customer Details

Name :

Address:

Company:

Phone:

Email :

Order Details

	#	Item/Description	Qty	Price	Discount	Total
☐						
☐						
☐						
☐						
☐						
☐						
☐						
☐						
☐						
☐						

TOTAL

Payment Details

Order :

Shipping :

Discount :

TAX :

Date

Total

Status

☐ Paid   ☐ Half Paid   ☐ Pending

Payment Method

☐ Cash   ☐ Credit Card   ☐ Bank   ☐ PayPal

☐ Other :

Special Notes

Delivery Details

Delivery Date :

Method : ☐ Pick-up   ☐ Delivery

Tracking No

Status

☐ Started   ☐ Finished   ☐ Delivered

Order Form

ORDER NO:

DATE:

ORDER NAME:

✓

Customer Details

Name :

Address:

Company:

Phone:

Email :

Order Details

	#	Item/Description	Qty	Price	Discount	Total
☐						
☐						
☐						
☐						
☐						
☐						
☐						
☐						
☐						
☐						

TOTAL

Payment Details

Order :

Shipping :

Discount :

TAX :

Date

Total

Status
☐ Paid ☐ Half Paid ☐ Pending

Payment Method
☐ Cash ☐ Credit Card ☐ Bank ☐ PayPal
☐ Other :

Delivery Details

Delivery Date :

Method : ☐ Pick-up ☐ Delivery

Tracking No

Status
☐ Started ☐ Finished ☐ Delivered

Special Notes

Order Form

ORDER NO:

DATE:

ORDER NAME:

✓

Customer Details

Name :

Company:

Phone:

Email :

Address:

Order Details

	#	Item/Description	Qty	Price	Discount	Total
☐						
☐						
☐						
☐						
☐						
☐						
☐						
☐						
☐						
☐						

TOTAL

Payment Details

Order :

Shipping :

Discount :

TAX :

Date

Total

Status

☐ Paid ☐ Half Paid ☐ Pending

Payment Method

☐ Cash ☐ Credit Card ☐ Bank ☐ PayPal

☐ Other :

Delivery Details

Delivery Date :

Method : ☐ Pick-up ☐ Delivery

Tracking No

Status

☐ Started ☐ Finished ☐ Delivered

Special Notes

Order Form

ORDER NO:

DATE:

ORDER NAME:

✓

Customer Details

Name :

Address:

Company:

Phone:

Email :

Order Details

	#	Item/Description	Qty	Price	Discount	Total
☐						
☐						
☐						
☐						
☐						
☐						
☐						
☐						
☐						
☐						

TOTAL

Payment Details

Order :

Shipping :

Discount :

TAX :

Date

Total

Status

☐ Paid   ☐ Half Paid   ☐ Pending

Payment Method

☐ Cash   ☐ Credit Card   ☐ Bank   ☐ PayPal

☐ Other :

Delivery Details

Delivery Date :

Method : ☐ Pick-up   ☐ Delivery

Tracking No

Status

☐ Started   ☐ Finished   ☐ Delivered

Special Notes

Order Form

ORDER NO:

DATE:

ORDER NAME:

✓

Customer Details

Name :

Address:

Company:

Phone:

Email :

Order Details

#	Item/Description	Qty	Price	Discount	Total
☐					
☐					
☐					
☐					
☐					
☐					
☐					
☐					
☐					
☐					

TOTAL

Payment Details

Order :

Shipping :

Discount :

TAX :

Date

Total

Status
☐ Paid   ☐ Half Paid   ☐ Pending

Payment Method
☐ Cash   ☐ Credit Card   ☐ Bank   ☐ PayPal
☐ Other :

Delivery Details

Delivery Date :

Method : ☐ Pick-up   ☐ Delivery

Tracking No

Status
☐ Started   ☐ Finished   ☐ Delivered

Special Notes

Order Form

ORDER NO:

DATE:

ORDER NAME:

✓

Customer Details

Name :

Company:

Phone: Email :

Address:

Order Details

	#	Item/Description	Qty	Price	Discount	Total
☐						
☐						
☐						
☐						
☐						
☐						
☐						
☐						
☐						
☐						

TOTAL

Payment Details

Order   :

Shipping :

Discount :

TAX   :

Date

Total

Status
☐ Paid   ☐ Half Paid   ☐ Pending

Payment Method
☐ Cash   ☐ Credit Card   ☐ Bank   ☐ PayPal
☐ Other :

Delivery Details

Delivery Date :

Method   :   ☐ Pick-up   ☐ Delivery

Tracking No

Status
☐ Started   ☐ Finished   ☐ Delivered

Special Notes

Order Form

ORDER NO:

DATE:

ORDER NAME:

✓

Customer Details

Name :

Address:

Company:

Phone:

Email :

Order Details

	#	Item/Description	Qty	Price	Discount	Total
☐						
☐						
☐						
☐						
☐						
☐						
☐						
☐						
☐						
☐						

TOTAL

Payment Details

Order :

Shipping :

Discount :

TAX :

Date

Total

Status

☐ Paid   ☐ Half Paid   ☐ Pending

Payment Method

☐ Cash   ☐ Credit Card   ☐ Bank   ☐ PayPal

☐ Other :

Special Notes

Delivery Details

Delivery Date :

Method : ☐ Pick-up   ☐ Delivery

Tracking No

Status

☐ Started   ☐ Finished   ☐ Delivered

Order Form

ORDER NO:

DATE:

ORDER NAME:

✓

Customer Details

Name : _____

Company: _____

Phone: _____

Email : _____

Address: _____
_____
_____

Order Details

#	Item/Description	Qty	Price	Discount	Total
☐					
☐					
☐					
☐					
☐					
☐					
☐					
☐					
☐					
☐					

TOTAL

Payment Details

Order : _____

Shipping : _____

Discount : _____

TAX : _____

Date

Total

Status

☐ Paid ☐ Half Paid ☐ Pending

Payment Method

☐ Cash ☐ Credit Card ☐ Bank ☐ PayPal

☐ Other : _____

Delivery Details

Delivery Date : _____

Method : ☐ Pick-up ☐ Delivery

Tracking No

Status

☐ Started ☐ Finished ☐ Delivered

Special Notes

Order Form

ORDER NO:

DATE:

ORDER NAME:

✓

Customer Details

Name :

Company:

Phone: Email :

Address:

Order Details

	#	Item/Description	Qty	Price	Discount	Total
☐						
☐						
☐						
☐						
☐						
☐						
☐						
☐						
☐						
☐						

TOTAL

Payment Details

Order   :

Shipping :

Discount :

TAX   :

Date

Total

Status

☐ Paid   ☐ Half Paid   ☐ Pending

Payment Method

☐ Cash   ☐ Credit Card   ☐ Bank   ☐ PayPal

☐ Other :

Delivery Details

Delivery Date :

Method   :   ☐ Pick-up   ☐ Delivery

Tracking No

Status

☐ Started   ☐ Finished   ☐ Delivered

Special Notes

Order Form

ORDER NO:

DATE:

ORDER NAME:

✓

Customer Details

Name :

Company:

Phone:

Email :

Address:

Order Details

#	Item/Description	Qty	Price	Discount	Total
☐					
☐					
☐					
☐					
☐					
☐					
☐					
☐					
☐					
☐					

TOTAL

Payment Details

Order :

Shipping :

Discount :

TAX :

Date

Total

Status

☐ Paid ☐ Half Paid ☐ Pending

Payment Method

☐ Cash ☐ Credit Card ☐ Bank ☐ PayPal

☐ Other :

Special Notes

Delivery Details

Delivery Date :

Method : ☐ Pick-up ☐ Delivery

Tracking No

Status

☐ Started ☐ Finished ☐ Delivered

Order Form

ORDER NO:

DATE:

ORDER NAME:

✓

Customer Details

Name : _____

Company: _____

Phone: _____ Email : _____

Address: _____
_____

Order Details

#	Item/Description	Qty	Price	Discount	Total
☐					
☐					
☐					
☐					
☐					
☐					
☐					
☐					
☐					
☐					

TOTAL

Payment Details

Order : _____

Shipping : _____

Discount : _____

TAX : _____

Date

Total

Status

☐ Paid ☐ Half Paid ☐ Pending

Payment Method

☐ Cash ☐ Credit Card ☐ Bank ☐ PayPal

☐ Other : _____

Delivery Details

Delivery Date : _____

Method : ☐ Pick-up ☐ Delivery

Tracking No

Status

☐ Started ☐ Finished ☐ Delivered

Special Notes

Order Form

ORDER NO:

DATE:

ORDER NAME:

✓

Customer Details

Name :

Address:

Company:

Phone:

Email :

Order Details

#	Item/Description	Qty	Price	Discount	Total
☐					
☐					
☐					
☐					
☐					
☐					
☐					
☐					
☐					
☐					

TOTAL

Payment Details

Order :

Shipping :

Discount :

TAX :

Date

Total

Status
☐ Paid ☐ Half Paid ☐ Pending

Payment Method
☐ Cash ☐ Credit Card ☐ Bank ☐ PayPal
☐ Other :

Delivery Details

Delivery Date :

Method : ☐ Pick-up ☐ Delivery

Tracking No

Status
☐ Started ☐ Finished ☐ Delivered

Special Notes

Order Form

ORDER NO:

DATE:

ORDER NAME:

✓

Customer Details

Name :

Address:

Company:

Phone:

Email :

Order Details

	#	Item/Description	Qty	Price	Discount	Total
☐						
☐						
☐						
☐						
☐						
☐						
☐						
☐						
☐						
☐						

TOTAL

Payment Details

Order :

Shipping :

Discount :

TAX :

Date

Total

Status
☐ Paid   ☐ Half Paid   ☐ Pending

Payment Method
☐ Cash   ☐ Credit Card   ☐ Bank   ☐ PayPal
☐ Other :

Delivery Details

Delivery Date :

Method : ☐ Pick-up ☐ Delivery

Tracking No

Status
☐ Started   ☐ Finished   ☐ Delivered

Special Notes

Order Form

ORDER NO:

DATE:

ORDER NAME:

✓

Customer Details

Name :

Company:

Phone:

Email :

Address:

Order Details

	#	Item/Description	Qty	Price	Discount	Total
☐						
☐						
☐						
☐						
☐						
☐						
☐						
☐						
☐						
☐						

TOTAL

Payment Details

Order :

Shipping :

Discount :

TAX :

Date

Total

Status
☐ Paid ☐ Half Paid ☐ Pending

Payment Method
☐ Cash ☐ Credit Card ☐ Bank ☐ PayPal
☐ Other :

Delivery Details

Delivery Date :

Method : ☐ Pick-up ☐ Delivery

Tracking No

Status
☐ Started ☐ Finished ☐ Delivered

Special Notes

Order Form

ORDER NO:

DATE:

ORDER NAME:

✓

Customer Details

Name :

Company:

Phone:

Email :

Address:

Order Details

#	Item/Description	Qty	Price	Discount	Total
☐					
☐					
☐					
☐					
☐					
☐					
☐					
☐					
☐					
☐					
				TOTAL	

Payment Details

Order :

Shipping :

Discount :

TAX :

Date

Total

Status

☐ Paid   ☐ Half Paid   ☐ Pending

Payment Method

☐ Cash   ☐ Credit Card   ☐ Bank   ☐ PayPal

☐ Other :

Delivery Details

Delivery Date :

Method : ☐ Pick-up   ☐ Delivery

Tracking No

Status

☐ Started   ☐ Finished   ☐ Delivered

Special Notes

Order Form

ORDER NO:

DATE:

ORDER NAME:

✓

Customer Details

Name :

Company:

Phone:

Email :

Address:

Order Details

#	Item/Description	Qty	Price	Discount	Total
☐					
☐					
☐					
☐					
☐					
☐					
☐					
☐					
☐					
☐					

TOTAL

Payment Details

Order :

Shipping :

Discount :

TAX :

Date

Total

Status

☐ Paid ☐ Half Paid ☐ Pending

Payment Method

☐ Cash ☐ Credit Card ☐ Bank ☐ PayPal

☐ Other :

Delivery Details

Delivery Date :

Method : ☐ Pick-up ☐ Delivery

Tracking No

Status

☐ Started ☐ Finished ☐ Delivered

Special Notes

Order Form

ORDER NO:

DATE:

ORDER NAME:

✓

Customer Details

Name :

Company:

Phone:

Address:

Email :

Order Details

	#	Item/Description	Qty	Price	Discount	Total
☐						
☐						
☐						
☐						
☐						
☐						
☐						
☐						
☐						
☐						

TOTAL

Payment Details

Order :

Shipping :

Discount :

TAX :

Date

Total

Status

☐ Paid   ☐ Half Paid   ☐ Pending

Payment Method

☐ Cash ☐ Credit Card ☐ Bank ☐ PayPal

☐ Other :

Delivery Details

Delivery Date :

Method   :   ☐ Pick-up   ☐ Delivery

Tracking No

Status

☐ Started   ☐ Finished   ☐ Delivered

Special Notes

Order Form

ORDER NO:

DATE:

ORDER NAME:

✓

Customer Details

Name :

Company:

Phone:

Email :

Address:

Order Details

	#	Item/Description	Qty	Price	Discount	Total
☐						
☐						
☐						
☐						
☐						
☐						
☐						
☐						
☐						
☐						

TOTAL

Payment Details

Order :

Shipping :

Discount :

TAX :

Date

Total

Status

☐ Paid   ☐ Half Paid   ☐ Pending

Payment Method

☐ Cash   ☐ Credit Card   ☐ Bank   ☐ PayPal

☐ Other :

Delivery Details

Delivery Date :

Method : ☐ Pick-up   ☐ Delivery

Tracking No

Status

☐ Started   ☐ Finished   ☐ Delivered

Special Notes

Order Form

ORDER NO:

DATE:

ORDER NAME:

✓

Customer Details

Name :

Company:

Phone:

Email :

Address:

Order Details

	#	Item/Description	Qty	Price	Discount	Total
☐						
☐						
☐						
☐						
☐						
☐						
☐						
☐						
☐						
☐						

TOTAL

Payment Details

Order :

Shipping :

Dicoount :

TAX :

Date

Total

Status
☐ Paid ☐ Half Paid ☐ Pending

Payment Method
☐ Cash ☐ Credit Card ☐ Bank ☐ PayPal
☐ Other :

Special Notes

Delivery Details

Delivery Date :

Method : ☐ Pick-up ☐ Delivery

Tracking No

Status
☐ Started ☐ Finished ☐ Delivered

Order Form

ORDER NO:

DATE:

ORDER NAME:

✓

Customer Details

Name :

Address:

Company:

Phone:

Email :

Order Details

#	Item/Description	Qty	Price	Discount	Total
☐					
☐					
☐					
☐					
☐					
☐					
☐					
☐					
☐					
☐					
				TOTAL	

Payment Details

Order :

Shipping :

Discount :

TAX :

Date

Total

Status

☐ Paid ☐ Half Paid ☐ Pending

Payment Method

☐ Cash ☐ Credit Card ☐ Bank ☐ PayPal

☐ Other :

Delivery Details

Delivery Date :

Method : ☐ Pick-up ☐ Delivery

Tracking No

Status

☐ Started ☐ Finished ☐ Delivered

Special Notes

Order Form

ORDER NO:

DATE:

ORDER NAME:

✓

Customer Details

Name :

Address:

Company:

Phone:

Email :

Order Details

#	Item/Description	Qty	Price	Discount	Total
☐					
☐					
☐					
☐					
☐					
☐					
☐					
☐					
☐					
☐					

TOTAL

Payment Details

Order :

Shipping :

Discount :

TAX :

Date

Total

Status
☐ Paid ☐ Half Paid ☐ Pending

Payment Method
☐ Cash ☐ Credit Card ☐ Bank ☐ PayPal
☐ Other :

Special Notes

Delivery Details

Delivery Date :

Method : ☐ Pick-up ☐ Delivery

Tracking No

Status
☐ Started ☐ Finished ☐ Delivered

Order Form

ORDER NO:

DATE:

ORDER NAME:

✓

Customer Details

Name :

Company:

Phone: Email :

Address:

Order Details

	#	Item/Description	Qty	Price	Discount	Total
☐						
☐						
☐						
☐						
☐						
☐						
☐						
☐						
☐						
☐						

TOTAL

Payment Details

Order   :

Shipping :

Discount :

TAX   :

Date

Total

Status

☐ Paid   ☐ Half Paid   ☐ Pending

Payment Method

☐ Cash   ☐ Credit Card   ☐ Bank   ☐ PayPal

☐ Other :

Delivery Details

Delivery Date :

Method   :   ☐ Pick-up   ☐ Delivery

Tracking No

Status

☐ Started   ☐ Finished   ☐ Delivered

Special Notes

Order Form

ORDER NO:

DATE:

ORDER NAME:

✓

Customer Details

Name :

Company:

Phone:

Email :

Address:

Order Details

	#	Item/Description	Qty	Price	Discount	Total
☐						
☐						
☐						
☐						
☐						
☐						
☐						
☐						
☐						
☐						

TOTAL

Payment Details

Order :

Shipping :

Discount :

TAX :

Date

Total

Status
☐ Paid ☐ Half Paid ☐ Pending

Payment Method
☐ Cash ☐ Credit Card ☐ Bank ☐ PayPal
☐ Other :

Delivery Details

Delivery Date :

Method : ☐ Pick-up ☐ Delivery

Tracking No

Status
☐ Started ☐ Finished ☐ Delivered

Special Notes

Order Form

ORDER NO:

DATE:

ORDER NAME:

✓

Customer Details

Name :

Company:

Phone:

Email :

Address:

Order Details

	#	Item/Description	Qty	Price	Discount	Total
☐						
☐						
☐						
☐						
☐						
☐						
☐						
☐						
☐						
☐						

TOTAL

Payment Details

Order :

Shipping :

Discount :

TAX :

Date

Total

Status

☐ Paid ☐ Half Paid ☐ Pending

Payment Method

☐ Cash ☐ Credit Card ☐ Bank ☐ PayPal

☐ Other :

Delivery Details

Delivery Date :

Method : ☐ Pick-up ☐ Delivery

Tracking No

Status

☐ Started ☐ Finished ☐ Delivered

Special Notes

Order Form

ORDER NO:

DATE:

ORDER NAME:

✓

Customer Details

Name :

Company:

Phone:

Email :

Address:

Order Details

	#	Item/Description	Qty	Price	Discount	Total
☐						
☐						
☐						
☐						
☐						
☐						
☐						
☐						
☐						
☐						

TOTAL

Payment Details

Order :

Shipping :

Discount :

TAX :

Date

Total

Status

☐ Paid　☐ Half Paid　☐ Pending

Payment Method

☐ Cash　☐ Credit Card　☐ Bank　☐ PayPal

☐ Other :

Special Notes

Delivery Details

Delivery Date :

Method : ☐ Pick-up　☐ Delivery

Tracking No

Status

☐ Started　☐ Finished　☐ Delivered

Order Form

ORDER NO:

DATE:

ORDER NAME:

✓

Customer Details

Name :

Address:

Company:

Phone:

Email :

Order Details

	#	Item/Description	Qty	Price	Discount	Total
☐						
☐						
☐						
☐						
☐						
☐						
☐						
☐						
☐						
☐						
					TOTAL	

Payment Details

Order :

Shipping :

Discount :

TAX :

Date

Total

Status

☐ Paid   ☐ Half Paid   ☐ Pending

Payment Method

☐ Cash   ☐ Credit Card   ☐ Bank   ☐ PayPal

☐ Other :

Special Notes

Delivery Details

Delivery Date :

Method : ☐ Pick-up   ☐ Delivery

Tracking No

Status

☐ Started   ☐ Finished   ☐ Delivered

Order Form

ORDER NO:

DATE:

ORDER NAME:

✓

Customer Details

Name :

Address:

Company:

Phone:

Email :

Order Details

	#	Item/Description	Qty	Price	Discount	Total
☐						
☐						
☐						
☐						
☐						
☐						
☐						
☐						
☐						
☐						

TOTAL

Payment Details

Order :

Shipping :

Discount :

TAX :

Date

Total

Status
☐ Paid ☐ Half Paid ☐ Pending

Payment Method
☐ Cash ☐ Credit Card ☐ Bank ☐ PayPal
☐ Other :

Special Notes

Delivery Details

Delivery Date :

Method : ☐ Pick-up ☐ Delivery

Tracking No

Status
☐ Started ☐ Finished ☐ Delivered

Order Form

ORDER NO:

DATE:

ORDER NAME:

✓

Customer Details

Name : _____

Company: _____

Phone: _____

Email : _____

Address: _____

_____

_____

Order Details

	#	Item/Description	Qty	Price	Discount	Total
☐						
☐						
☐						
☐						
☐						
☐						
☐						
☐						
☐						
☐						

TOTAL

Payment Details

Order : _____

Shipping : _____

Discount : _____

TAX : _____

Date

Total

Status

☐ Paid   ☐ Half Paid   ☐ Pending

Payment Method

☐ Cash   ☐ Credit Card   ☐ Bank   ☐ PayPal

☐ Other : _____

Special Notes

Delivery Details

Delivery Date : _____

Method : ☐ Pick-up   ☐ Delivery

Tracking No

Status

☐ Started   ☐ Finished   ☐ Delivered

Order Form

ORDER NO:

DATE:

ORDER NAME:

✓

Customer Details

Name :

Company:

Phone:

Email :

Address:

Order Details

	#	Item/Description	Qty	Price	Discount	Total
☐						
☐						
☐						
☐						
☐						
☐						
☐						
☐						
☐						
☐						

TOTAL

Payment Details

Order :

Shipping :

Discount :

TAX :

Date

Total

Status
☐ Paid   ☐ Half Paid   ☐ Pending

Payment Method
☐ Cash   ☐ Credit Card   ☐ Bank   ☐ PayPal
☐ Other :

Special Notes

Delivery Details

Delivery Date :

Method : ☐ Pick-up   ☐ Delivery

Tracking No

Status
☐ Started   ☐ Finished   ☐ Delivered

Order Form

ORDER NO:

DATE:

ORDER NAME:

✓

Customer Details

Name :

Company:

Phone:

Email :

Address:

Order Details

#	Item/Description	Qty	Price	Discount	Total
☐					
☐					
☐					
☐					
☐					
☐					
☐					
☐					
☐					
☐					

TOTAL

Payment Details

Order :

Shipping :

Discount :

TAX :

Date

Total

Status

☐ Paid   ☐ Half Paid   ☐ Pending

Payment Method

☐ Cash   ☐ Credit Card   ☐ Bank   ☐ PayPal

☐ Other :

Special Notes

Delivery Details

Delivery Date :

Method : ☐ Pick-up   ☐ Delivery

Tracking No

Status

☐ Started   ☐ Finished   ☐ Delivered

Order Form

ORDER NO:

DATE:

ORDER NAME:

✓

Customer Details

Name :

Company:

Phone:

Email :

Address:

Order Details

	#	Item/Description	Qty	Price	Discount	Total
☐						
☐						
☐						
☐						
☐						
☐						
☐						
☐						
☐						
☐						

TOTAL

Payment Details

Order :

Shipping :

Discount :

TAX :

Date

Total

Status

☐ Paid ☐ Half Paid ☐ Pending

Payment Method

☐ Cash ☐ Credit Card ☐ Bank ☐ PayPal

☐ Other :

Special Notes

Delivery Details

Delivery Date :

Method : ☐ Pick-up ☐ Delivery

Tracking No

Status

☐ Started ☐ Finished ☐ Delivered

Order Form

ORDER NO:

DATE:

ORDER NAME:

✓

Customer Details

Name :

Address:

Company:

Phone:

Email :

Order Details

#	Item/Description	Qty	Price	Discount	Total
☐					
☐					
☐					
☐					
☐					
☐					
☐					
☐					
☐					
☐					

TOTAL

Payment Details

Order :

Shipping :

Discount :

TAX :

Date

Total

Status

☐ Paid ☐ Half Paid ☐ Pending

Payment Method

☐ Cash ☐ Credit Card ☐ Bank ☐ PayPal

☐ Other :

Special Notes

Delivery Details

Delivery Date :

Method : ☐ Pick-up ☐ Delivery

Tracking No

Status

☐ Started ☐ Finished ☐ Delivered

Order Form

ORDER NO:

DATE:

ORDER NAME:

✓

Customer Details

Name :

Company:

Phone:

Email :

Address:

Order Details

	#	Item/Description	Qty	Price	Discount	Total
☐						
☐						
☐						
☐						
☐						
☐						
☐						
☐						
☐						
☐						

TOTAL

Payment Details

Order :

Shipping :

Discount :

TAX :

Date

Total

Status

☐ Paid ☐ Half Paid ☐ Pending

Payment Method

☐ Cash ☐ Credit Card ☐ Bank ☐ PayPal

☐ Other :

Special Notes

Delivery Details

Delivery Date :

Method : ☐ Pick-up ☐ Delivery

Tracking No

Status

☐ Started ☐ Finished ☐ Delivered

Order Form

ORDER NO:

DATE:

ORDER NAME:

✓

Customer Details

Name :

Address:

Company:

Phone:

Email :

Order Details

	#	Item/Description	Qty	Price	Discount	Total
☐						
☐						
☐						
☐						
☐						
☐						
☐						
☐						
☐						
☐						

TOTAL

Payment Details

Order :

Shipping :

Discount :

TAX :

Date

Total

Status

☐ Paid ☐ Half Paid ☐ Pending

Payment Method

☐ Cash ☐ Credit Card ☐ Bank ☐ PayPal

☐ Other :

Delivery Details

Delivery Date :

Method : ☐ Pick-up ☐ Delivery

Tracking No

Status

☐ Started ☐ Finished ☐ Delivered

Special Notes

Order Form

ORDER NO:

DATE:

ORDER NAME:

✓

Customer Details

Name :

Company:

Phone:

Email :

Address:

Order Details

	#	Item/Description	Qty	Price	Discount	Total
☐						
☐						
☐						
☐						
☐						
☐						
☐						
☐						
☐						
☐						

TOTAL

Payment Details

Order :

Shipping :

Discount :

TAX :

Date

Total

Status

☐ Paid   ☐ Half Paid   ☐ Pending

Payment Method

☐ Cash   ☐ Credit Card   ☐ Bank   ☐ PayPal

☐ Other :

Special Notes

Delivery Details

Delivery Date :

Method : ☐ Pick-up   ☐ Delivery

Tracking No

Status

☐ Started   ☐ Finished   ☐ Delivered

Order Form

ORDER NO:

DATE:

ORDER NAME:

✓

Customer Details

Name : _____

Company: _____

Phone: _____

Email : _____

Address: _____

_____

_____

Order Details

☐	#	Item/Description	Qty	Price	Discount	Total
☐						
☐						
☐						
☐						
☐						
☐						
☐						
☐						
☐						
☐						

TOTAL

Payment Details

Order : _____

Shipping : _____

Discount : _____

TAX : _____

Date

Total

Status

☐ Paid   ☐ Half Paid   ☐ Pending

Payment Method

☐ Cash   ☐ Credit Card   ☐ Bank   ☐ PayPal

☐ Other : _____

Special Notes

Delivery Details

Delivery Date : _____

Method : ☐ Pick-up   ☐ Delivery

Tracking No

Status

☐ Started   ☐ Finished   ☐ Delivered

Order Form

ORDER NO:

DATE:

ORDER NAME:

✓

Customer Details

Name :

Company:

Phone:

Email :

Address:

Order Details

	#	Item/Description	Qty	Price	Discount	Total
☐						
☐						
☐						
☐						
☐						
☐						
☐						
☐						
☐						
☐						

TOTAL

Payment Details

Order :

Shipping :

Discount :

TAX :

Date

Total

Status

☐ Paid ☐ Half Paid ☐ Pending

Payment Method

☐ Cash ☐ Credit Card ☐ Bank ☐ PayPal

☐ Other :

Special Notes

Delivery Details

Delivery Date :

Method : ☐ Pick-up ☐ Delivery

Tracking No

Status

☐ Started ☐ Finished ☐ Delivered

Order Form

ORDER NO:

DATE:

ORDER NAME:

✓

Customer Details

Name :

Company:

Phone:

Email :

Address:

Order Details

	#	Item/Description	Qty	Price	Discount	Total
☐						
☐						
☐						
☐						
☐						
☐						
☐						
☐						
☐						
☐						

TOTAL

Payment Details

Order :

Shipping :

Discount :

TAX :

Date

Total

Status

☐ Paid ☐ Half Paid ☐ Pending

Payment Method

☐ Cash ☐ Credit Card ☐ Bank ☐ PayPal

☐ Other :

Delivery Details

Delivery Date :

Method : ☐ Pick-up ☐ Delivery

Tracking No

Status

☐ Started ☐ Finished ☐ Delivered

Special Notes

Order Form

ORDER NO:

DATE:

ORDER NAME:

✓

Customer Details

Name :

Address:

Company:

Phone:

Email :

Order Details

	#	Item/Description	Qty	Price	Discount	Total
☐						
☐						
☐						
☐						
☐						
☐						
☐						
☐						
☐						
☐						
					TOTAL	

Payment Details

Order :

Shipping :

Discount :

TAX :

Date

Total

Status

☐ Paid   ☐ Half Paid   ☐ Pending

Payment Method

☐ Cash   ☐ Credit Card   ☐ Bank   ☐ PayPal

☐ Other :

Delivery Details

Delivery Date :

Method : ☐ Pick-up   ☐ Delivery

Tracking No

Status

☐ Started   ☐ Finished   ☐ Delivered

Special Notes

Order Form

ORDER NO:

DATE:

ORDER NAME:

✓

Customer Details

Name :

Address:

Company:

Phone:

Email :

Order Details

	#	Item/Description	Qty	Price	Discount	Total
☐						
☐						
☐						
☐						
☐						
☐						
☐						
☐						
☐						
☐						

TOTAL

Payment Details

Order :

Shipping :

Discount :

TAX :

Date

Total

Status

☐ Paid   ☐ Half Paid   ☐ Pending

Payment Method

☐ Cash   ☐ Credit Card   ☐ Bank   ☐ PayPal

☐ Other :

Delivery Details

Delivery Date :

Method : ☐ Pick-up   ☐ Delivery

Tracking No

Status

☐ Started   ☐ Finished   ☐ Delivered

Special Notes

Order Form

ORDER NO:

DATE:

ORDER NAME:

✓

Customer Details

Name :

Address:

Company:

Phone:

Email :

Order Details

	#	Item/Description	Qty	Price	Discount	Total
☐						
☐						
☐						
☐						
☐						
☐						
☐						
☐						
☐						
☐						

TOTAL

Payment Details

Order :

Shipping :

Discount :

TAX :

Date

Total

Status

☐ Paid ☐ Half Paid ☐ Pending

Payment Method

☐ Cash ☐ Credit Card ☐ Bank ☐ PayPal

☐ Other :

Delivery Details

Delivery Date :

Method : ☐ Pick-up ☐ Delivery

Tracking No

Status

☐ Started ☐ Finished ☐ Delivered

Special Notes

Order Form

ORDER NO:

DATE:

ORDER NAME: ✓

Customer Details

Name :   Address:

Company:

Phone: Email :

Order Details

	#	Item/Description	Qty	Price	Discount	Total
☐						
☐						
☐						
☐						
☐						
☐						
☐						
☐						
☐						
☐						

TOTAL

Payment Details

Order   :

Shipping :

Discount :

TAX   :

Date

Total

Status
☐ Paid   ☐ Half Paid   ☐ Pending

Payment Method
☐ Cash ☐ Credit Card ☐ Bank ☐ PayPal
☐ Other :

Special Notes

Delivery Details

Delivery Date :

Method   : ☐ Pick-up ☐ Delivery

Tracking No

Status
☐ Started   ☐ Finished   ☐ Delivered

Order Form

ORDER NO:

DATE:

ORDER NAME:

✓

Customer Details

Name :

Address:

Company:

Phone:

Email :

Order Details

	#	Item/Description	Qty	Price	Discount	Total
☐						
☐						
☐						
☐						
☐						
☐						
☐						
☐						
☐						
☐						

TOTAL

Payment Details

Order :

Shipping :

Discount :

TAX :

Date

Total

Status

☐ Paid ☐ Half Paid ☐ Pending

Payment Method

☐ Cash ☐ Credit Card ☐ Bank ☐ PayPal

☐ Other :

Delivery Details

Delivery Date :

Method : ☐ Pick-up ☐ Delivery

Tracking No

Status

☐ Started ☐ Finished ☐ Delivered

Special Notes

Order Form

ORDER NO:

DATE:

ORDER NAME:

✓

Customer Details

Name :

Company:

Phone:

Email :

Address:

Order Details

	#	Item/Description	Qty	Price	Discount	Total
☐						
☐						
☐						
☐						
☐						
☐						
☐						
☐						
☐						
☐						

TOTAL

Payment Details

Order   :

Shipping :

Discount :

TAX   :

Date

Total

Status
☐ Paid   ☐ Half Paid   ☐ Pending

Payment Method
☐ Cash   ☐ Credit Card   ☐ Bank   ☐ PayPal
☐ Other :

Delivery Details

Delivery Date :

Method   :   ☐ Pick-up   ☐ Delivery

Tracking No

Status
☐ Started   ☐ Finished   ☐ Delivered

Special Notes

Order Form

ORDER NO:

DATE:

ORDER NAME:

✓

Customer Details

Name :

Company:

Phone:

Email :

Address:

Order Details

	#	Item/Description	Qty	Price	Discount	Total
☐						
☐						
☐						
☐						
☐						
☐						
☐						
☐						
☐						
☐						

TOTAL

Payment Details

Order :

Shipping :

Discount :

TAX :

Date

Total

Status

☐ Paid ☐ Half Paid ☐ Pending

Payment Method

☐ Cash ☐ Credit Card ☐ Bank ☐ PayPal

☐ Other :

Delivery Details

Delivery Date :

Method : ☐ Pick-up ☐ Delivery

Tracking No

Status

☐ Started ☐ Finished ☐ Delivered

Special Notes

Order Form

ORDER NO:

DATE:

ORDER NAME:

✓

Customer Details

Name :

Company:

Phone:

Email :

Address:

Order Details

	#	Item/Description	Qty	Price	Discount	Total
☐						
☐						
☐						
☐						
☐						
☐						
☐						
☐						
☐						
☐						

TOTAL

Payment Details

Order :

Shipping :

Discount :

TAX :

Date

Total

Status
☐ Paid   ☐ Half Paid   ☐ Pending

Payment Method
☐ Cash   ☐ Credit Card   ☐ Bank   ☐ PayPal
☐ Other :

Delivery Details

Delivery Date :

Method : ☐ Pick-up   ☐ Delivery

Tracking No

Status
☐ Started   ☐ Finished   ☐ Delivered

Special Notes

Order Form

ORDER NO:

DATE:

ORDER NAME:

✓

Customer Details

Name :

Company:

Phone:

Email :

Address:

Order Details

#	Item/Description	Qty	Price	Discount	Total
☐					
☐					
☐					
☐					
☐					
☐					
☐					
☐					
☐					
☐					

TOTAL

Payment Details

Order :

Shipping :

Discount :

TAX :

Date

Total

Status

☐ Paid ☐ Half Paid ☐ Pending

Payment Method

☐ Cash ☐ Credit Card ☐ Bank ☐ PayPal

☐ Other :

Delivery Details

Delivery Date :

Method : ☐ Pick-up ☐ Delivery

Tracking No

Status

☐ Started ☐ Finished ☐ Delivered

Special Notes

Order Form

ORDER NO:

DATE:

ORDER NAME:

✓

Customer Details

Name : _____

Address: _____

Company: _____

_____

Phone: _____

Email : _____

_____

Order Details

	#	Item/Description	Qty	Price	Discount	Total
☐						
☐						
☐						
☐						
☐						
☐						
☐						
☐						
☐						
☐						

TOTAL

Payment Details

Order : _____

Shipping : _____

Discount : _____

TAX : _____

Date

Total

Status

☐ Paid   ☐ Half Paid   ☐ Pending

Payment Method

☐ Cash   ☐ Credit Card   ☐ Bank   ☐ PayPal

☐ Other : _____

Delivery Details

Delivery Date : _____

Method : ☐ Pick-up   ☐ Delivery

Tracking No

Status

☐ Started   ☐ Finished   ☐ Delivered

Special Notes

Order Form

ORDER NO:

DATE:

ORDER NAME:

✓

Customer Details

Name :

Company:

Phone:

Email :

Address:

Order Details

	#	Item/Description	Qty	Price	Discount	Total
☐						
☐						
☐						
☐						
☐						
☐						
☐						
☐						
☐						
☐						

TOTAL

Payment Details

Order :

Shipping :

Discount :

TAX :

Date

Total

Status

☐ Paid   ☐ Half Paid   ☐ Pending

Payment Method

☐ Cash   ☐ Credit Card   ☐ Bank   ☐ PayPal

☐ Other :

Delivery Details

Delivery Date :

Method : ☐ Pick-up   ☐ Delivery

Tracking No

Status

☐ Started   ☐ Finished   ☐ Delivered

Special Notes

Order Form

ORDER NO:

DATE:

ORDER NAME:

✓

Customer Details

Name :

Address:

Company:

Phone: Email :

Order Details

☐	#	Item/Description	Qty	Price	Discount	Total
☐						
☐						
☐						
☐						
☐						
☐						
☐						
☐						
☐						
☐						

TOTAL

Payment Details

Order   :

Shipping :

Discount :

TAX   :

Date

Total

Status

☐ Paid   ☐ Half Paid   ☐ Pending

┌─ **Payment Method** ─┐

☐ Cash   ☐ Credit Card   ☐ Bank   ☐ PayPal

☐ Other :

Delivery Details

Delivery Date :

Method   :   ☐ Pick-up   ☐ Delivery

┌─ **Tracking No** ─┐   ┌─ **Status** ─┐

☐ Started   ☐ Finished   ☐ Delivered

Special Notes

Notes

Notes

Notes

Made in the USA
Las Vegas, NV
09 February 2022